To Savannah,
Sierra, Scarlett,
Hudson and Hunter,

Christopher Newport
discovered Jamestown, Virginia.
Enjoy his true story.

Sharon R. Solomon

CHRISTOPHER NEWPORT

CHRISTOPHER NEWPORT

Jamestown Explorer

By Sharon K. Solomon

Illustrated by Dan Bridy

PELICAN PUBLISHING COMPANY
GRETNA 2013

To my grandchildren Ella, Brady and Luke who learned about
Christopher Newport in school—SKS

The word "Pelican" and the depiction of a pelican are
trademarks of Pelican Publishing Company, Inc., and are
registered in the U.S. Patent and Trademark Office.

Library of Congress Cataloging-in-Publication Data

Solomon, Sharon K.
  Christopher Newport : Jamestown explorer / by Sharon K. Solomon ; illustrated by Dan Bridy.
    p. cm.
  ISBN 978-1-4556-1752-4 (hardcover : alk. paper) — ISBN 978-1-4556-1753-1 (e-book) 1. Newport, Christopher, ca. 1565-1617—Juvenile literature. 2. Virginia—Discovery and exploration—Juvenile literature. 3. Explorers—Virginia—Biography—Juvenile literature. 4. Explorers—Great Britain—Biography—Juvenile literature. 5. Virginia—History—Colonial period, ca. 1600-1775—Juvenile literature. 6. Jamestown (Va.)—History—Juvenile literature. 7. Ship captains—Great Britain—Biography—Juvenile literature. I. Bridy, Dan, ill. II. Title.
  F229.N48 S68 2013
  975.5'01092—dc23
  [B]
                      2012041933

Printed in Malaysia
Published by Pelican Publishing Company, Inc.
1000 Burmaster Street, Gretna, Louisiana 70053

Early Life
Born 1561, Harwich, England

Who would ever think that a young lad from Harwich, England, would change the world?

That boy was Christopher Newport, who grew up by the sea and spent much of his childhood on his father's ship. Just how did Christopher Newport change the world?

After sailing on trading vessels, Newport was hired to sail with Sir Francis Drake to capture Spanish ships and bring back precious treasures to England. Newport decided to become a privateer, just like Sir Francis.

The Spaniards called them pirates, but the English called themselves privateers. With the war going on between England and Spain, Queen Elizabeth was delighted when British sailors raided enemy ships and brought back riches to England.

Privateer
1587

The Drake expedition of 1587 to Cadiz, Spain, gave Newport a taste of victory and adventure. Three years later, in 1590 the owners of the ship *Little John* hired Newport to bring back gold, silver, and jewels from Spanish and Portuguese colonies in the West Indies. They also asked Newport to rescue the people of Roanoke, the first English colony in America.

Just as the *Little John* neared the island of Cuba, the crew spotted two Spanish treasure ships coming from Mexico. During a fight with the Spaniards, Newport had his right forearm cut off. Five crew members were killed and many others injured. When Newport's fleet got to Roanoke, they found no one!

In 1592 Newport took a job as captain of the *Golden Dragon*. Using his left hand to hold his sword, Newport and his crew captured nineteen Spanish ships in the West Indies.

On his way home, Newport spotted a large Portuguese ship, the *Madre de Dios,* on its way home from India with silks, spices, gold, and jewels worth a fortune. The crew drew their swords and defeated the *Madre de Dios*.

Newport spent the next ten years as a privateer until King James made peace with Spain. On one voyage, he brought back baby crocodiles for the king!

New World Mariner
1606, London, England

The Virginia Company wanted to establish English colonies in America. King James also wanted to find gold and silver and the Northwest Passage to China. Newport wanted to be the person to accomplish this. Because of his experience, Newport was chosen to command three ships controlled by the Virginia Company. This would be a really big adventure!

Newport and his crew used instruments to stay on course during the voyage across the Atlantic Ocean. The helmsman used a compass to mark off the direction every half-hour and the masters and Newport used navigational charts.

The cross staff was used to determine latitude. The astrolabe was used to observe the sun and moon's position. It was important to stay on course and know their ships' positions at all times.

Newport and 144 men and boys set off for America on the *Susan Constant*, the *Godspeed*, and the *Discovery*. One of the passengers, Captain John Smith, angered many of the men. Newport kept peace because of Smith's experience.

Newport sailed the southern route just as Christopher Columbus had done more than one hundred years before. The ships made stops in the West Indies where the Englishmen traded knives, hatchets, beads, and copper for food and tobacco.

In the Virgin Islands, the fleet anchored in the harbor and feasted on iguanas, tortoises, parrots, and fish.

The Virginia Company had directed Captain Newport to find a deep harbor set inland to protect it from enemies. The ships arrived along the coast of Virginia on April 26, 1607. That night they anchored their ship in the Chesapeake Bay and were attacked by Indians. Captain John Smith later wrote, "Captain Newport made a shot at them, which the Indians respected, but having spent their arrows, retired without harme."

It took many days of exploring inlets to find the right harbor. When Newport found this harbor on May 14, 1607, he named it Jamestown for His Majesty, King James.

Jamestown became the first permanent English-speaking colony in America. Establishing a colony in Virginia was not easy. Following instructions from the Virginia Company, they formed a government; then, they had to build houses and plant crops. Newport stayed long enough to meet some of the Powhatan tribes and explore the James River.

Between 1607 and 1611, Newport made four more voyages back to Jamestown. The colony needed supplies and more colonists to keep it thriving.

On his second voyage, Newport found Jamestown in horrible condition. Many of the men had died over the long, cold winter and others looked barely alive from lack of food. The new supplies and people helped the struggling colonists, but Newport needed to ask the Powhatans for help.

He presented gifts to Powhatan, the supreme chief, from King James. After that, Powhatan was willing to trade food for English tools. By the time Newport left Jamestown the second time, he had befriended the Powhatans and left the colony with more men and supplies.

On the third voyage, Newport brought more supplies and this time some women as well as men to live in Jamestown.

On the fourth mission in 1609, Newport and his crew were caught in a powerful hurricane near the island of Bermuda. Fearing that the ship would capsize, he steered it between two boulders where it crashed into pieces.

Life on Bermuda was another adventure. The captain, crew, and passengers lived off fish from the sea and berries and wild hogs found on the island.

They built two smaller ships with wood from the wrecked ship and made their way back to Jamestown nine months later in May 1610.

In 1611, on his fifth and final voyage to Jamestown, Newport found the colony in much better condition. There were many families and the colonists had learned to hunt and fish.

He never found the Northwest Passage to China or the gold, but Newport knew that his work in Jamestown was complete.

Epilogue
1611, London, England

Newport took a job with the East India Company. He made three trips to India and the East Indies and brought back valuable spices, cloth, and treasures. Newport's ship, the *Hope*, arrived in England on September 1, 1618 with the news of his death in Indonesia.

His navigational skills enabled Jamestown to become the first permanent English-speaking colony in America. This set the stage for more English colonies in America. Christopher Newport had indeed changed the world.

A Christopher Newport Timeline

1561: Newport is born in Harwich, England.

1581: Newport sails to Brazil aboard the *Minion*.

1589: Newport is Master of the *Margaret*.

1592: Newport sails in the *Golden Dragon* to the West Indies, and on the return trip he captures treasure from the *Madre de Dios*.

1605: Newport sails to the West Indies and brings back baby crocodiles for King James.

1606: Newport is "Principal Master of the Navy"; he is hired by the Virginia Company to find a site for a colony in Virginia.

1607: Newport arrives in Virginia on the *Susan Constant*; he returns to England and then makes a second voyage to Jamestown.

1608: Newport makes a third trip to Jamestown.

1609: Newport makes a fourth voyage to Jamestown; his ship is wrecked on the island of Bermuda in a hurricane; he arrives in Jamestown in May 1610.

1611: Newport's fifth and final trip to Jamestown; Shakespeare writes the play *The Tempest* partially based on Newport's shipwreck in 1609.

1612: Newport joins the East India Company, sails to the East Indies, and returns in 1614.

1615: Newport makes a second voyage to the East Indies, returning in 1616.

1616: Newport sails a third time to the East Indies; he dies in Bantam, Indonesia, in August 1617.

Glossary

apprentice—a beginner who may work for another to learn a trade

astrolabe—a round, heavy instrument used to measure altitude of the sun or stars and determine latitude

captain—the person in command of the ship

compass—an instrument showing direction (north, east, south, or west)

cross staff—an instrument to measure the angle above the horizon of the sun or stars to determine latitude

helmsman—the person who steers the ship

latitude—distance north or south of the equator

master—a person who directs the course and steering of the ship

privateer—a person who works on a ship hired by the government to attack and capture enemy ships during war time